Original title:
The Sea's Gentle Embrace

Copyright © 2025 Creative Arts Management OÜ
All rights reserved.

Author: Arabella Whitmore
ISBN HARDBACK: 978-1-80587-336-5
ISBN PAPERBACK: 978-1-80587-806-3

The Ocean's Breath of Repose

Waves crash down with a playful splash,
Seagulls squawk, they're quite the brash.
The sun shines bright on a bumbling crab,
Who dances oddly, oh what a kebab!

The starfish, lounging, wears quite a grin,
Saying, "Life's a beach; come take a spin!"
A fish flips down, does an odd little jig,
While a clam sings softly like a cow on a twig.

Swaying Between the Tides

A dolphin jumps, wearing shades of blue,
Doing flips while making fish stew.
The waves just chuckle, they know the score,
As jellyfish glide in a soft, blurred war.

Barnacles cling, though they want to dance,
But their slow-motion moves lack any chance.
Oh, the seaweed sways like a groovy band,
While crabs do the cha-cha, trying to stand!

Whispers of the Ocean

The wind whispers secrets, it tickles my ear,
As sea turtles giggle at my silly fear.
They call me close with a gentle 'hey there,'
As I trip on a wave, turning into a chair!

Shells gossip loudly on the sandy floor,
Spilling the tea that the tide can't ignore.
A fish in a tux holds a grand ball tonight,
While I flail about, just trying to take flight.

Tides of Tenderness

A crab in a hat takes a stroll on the sand,
While sea urchins watch as they're barely planned.
Lobsters with mustaches, oh what a sight,
Pinching and biting, then laughing outright.

The ocean grins wide, waves swirling in joy,
Tickling my toes like a playful little boy.
As sea foam hugs me, I can't help but laugh,
In this quirky realm, time's a silly giraffe!

Cradle of the Currents

Waves whisper secrets, oh what a jest,
They tickle my toes, I can't help but jest.
Fish swim in circles, a dance so absurd,
Their fins flapping wildly, haven't they heard?

This ocean's a joker, splashing with glee,
It steals all my snacks, that rascal, you see!
Salty and playful, it pulls me along,
As I dodge jellyfish, it sings me a song.

Soft Shores, Soft Hearts

On soft, sandy beaches, I build quite a thrill,
A tower of shells, or a fortress to fill.
But the tide has a plan, make no mistake,
It laughs at my castle, oh what a heartbreak!

Seagulls play guard, they squawk and they stare,
Plotting my downfall with casual flair.
But I laugh with the waves, for they're in on the joke,
While I dive for my flip-flops, the ocean just pokes.

Secrets Beneath the Foam

Under the bubbles, where crabs do their dance,
I spot a small octopus, lost in a trance.
He wiggles and giggles, with eight arms spread wide,
Who taught him ballet? I wish I could glide!

The fish all conspire, in colors so bright,
To prank on the swimmers, oh what a sight!
They flash and they dart, it's a colorful game,
While I splash in the shallows, they're plotting the same.

Love Letters on the Sand

With each passing wave, love notes appear,
Scrawled in the sand, a message so clear.
But as I lean closer, a gust sweeps it away,
A comical breeze, come spoil my grand play!

Shells sing their romance with a clink and a clatter,
While starfish look on, unmoved by the chatter.
Yet I can't help but chuckle, as each tide comes and goes,

For love here is playful, as anything knows.

Beneath the Azure Veil

Above the waves, a seagull flies,
Squawking loudly, it's quite a surprise.
A fish in a top hat swims with flair,
While seaweed dances without a care.

Turtles in shades look cool and slick,
Playing cards, they're quite the trick.
Crabs do the cha-cha on the sand,
Making mischief, oh it's quite grand.

Shores of Tranquil Dreams

On the beach, a clam tries to sing,
But ends up clattering, what a fling!
Starfish contort in a silly pose,
Wiggling their arms, as laughter grows.

A dolphin juggles fish with glee,
While me, I just spill my lemonade tea.
Seagulls steal fries from a sunbather's plate,
Oh, this holiday is truly first-rate!

Waves of Soothing Comfort

Surfboards flip like pancake stacks,
A surfer crashes, oh, what a whack!
Jellyfish jelly in the ocean sways,
While octopuses pull pranks for days.

Sandcastles crumble, kids start to squeal,
As a rogue wave comes to steal their meal.
Beach balls bounce with a boisterous cheer,
As all the fun unfolds, it's clear!

Glistening Heartbeats of the Deep

Goldfish parade with glittering scales,
In top hats and suits, tell fantastic tales.
A crab in a bowtie dances the night,
With a starfish partner that's quite a sight!

Bubbles rise up in a slippery whirl,
As fish play tag, giving tails a twirl.
Underwater laughter, oh what a scene,
In this wacky world, we all feel keen!

A Shoreline Sanctuary

Crabs in tuxedos, all dressed to dance,
Seagulls drop fries, they take a chance.
Waves chuckle softly, tickling my toes,
While starfish do yoga, striking new poses.

Kids build castles, but they just dissolve,
As I sip my drink, feeling resolve.
The tide pulls my worries right out of sight,
In this sandy abode, everything feels right.

Respite in the Blue

Fish have a party, they splash about,
While I try to sunbathe, I freak out.
A crab steals my sandwich, how rude can it be?
And dolphins are laughing, mocking at me.

In my inflatable, I float with a grin,
But watch that big wave—it's about to win!
I dip and I dive, the ocean's my stage,
Where humor and water turn every page.

Sunset's Tender Touch

Skies paint with orange, like nacho cheese,
I chase a lost beach ball, wishing for breeze.
Seagulls toast marshmallows, laughing away,
While the sun rolls down, it steals the day.

My shadow, a giant, does a silly jig,
As the crabs throw a rave, dancing so big.
On this wacky shore, I'm free and I play,
With nature's own antics brightening my day.

Reflections in the Tide

Mirrors of water, my hair's in a bun,
A jellyfish wobbles, but thinks it's so fun.
My laugh fills the air like waves hitting land,
While I gracefully trip, like it was all planned.

The tide whispers jokes, in a blue-hued laugh,
I chase chasing seagulls, they know my path.
With laughter and splashes, I make my own guide,
In this kooky world, I'll always abide.

Navigating Nurture

A crab on the shore with a starfish in tow,
Said, 'You're not my type, but let's take it slow!'
With flip-flops a-flap, I trip on a wave,
It laughs as I tumble, my grace it won't save.

Seagulls are squawking, they hold a great show,
With sandwiches stolen, they fly to and fro.
A fish waves goodbye, then flips with a splash,
While I chase my hat with a very sad dash.

The Gentle Hand of Nature

A dolphin winks at me, what a cheeky lad,
He tells all his friends that I'm simply mad.
With seaweed my crown, I dance to the beat,
The tide is my partner, but who has two left feet?

My toes in the sand, I summon a wave,
That mischievous ocean, oh, how it misbehaves!
A splash on my face, laughter fills the air,
I swear it just giggled; it's not even fair!

Breezes that Heal

A whispering breeze brings a tickle to me,
It plays with my hair, says 'Let's just be free!'
But as I leap high, on a gust of delight,
I tumble and roll; oh, what a funny sight!

The drifters abound, they all have their fun,
With kites and with laughter, we bask in the sun.
An octopus jives while I trip on my shoe,
He shrugs with a grin, as if he just knew.

Mysteries in the Mist

In the fog of the morn, as I squint through the haze,
A mermaid appears, and she's in quite a daze.
She offers me shells and a wild little tune,
While I muse on my toast, which I left with the moon.

The mystery thickens, what did I just see?
A crab wearing glasses, he stares back at me.
He scribbles with pencils and writes 'Life's a beach!',
And rolls back to the ocean, his words out of reach.

Embraced by the Briny Blue

The waves are laughing, what a sight,
A crab pinches toes, oh what a fright!
Seagulls squawk, they steal your fries,
While sand gets in your shorts - what a surprise!

The sun is shining, and so is my skin,
I think I'm glowing, where do I begin?
With sunscreen on my nose, I take a stand,
But the waves keep pulling me back to the sand!

Coastal Serenade of Stillness

Fish in the tide, are wearing a frown,
For fishermen's chores are bringing them down.
A clam plays hide and seek, oh what a tease,
While dolphins do flips, just to please!

Down by the docks, a seagull takes aim,
At lunch on the table, oh what a game!
With a clever swipe, it makes off with a bag,
Now who's got the last laugh, oh what a wag!

Refuge in the Ocean's Arms

The tide rolls in, with bubbles in tow,
While beach balls bounce, putting on a show.
The kids squeal with joy in their tiny sand pits,
Not knowing they'll soon be covered in bits!

A jellyfish floats by, with quite the flair,
But watch out, my friend, don't you dare touch that hair!
If you dance with the tides, just follow the beat,
For shells gather secrets beneath your feet!

Echoes of the Whispering Deep

Plankton throw parties, tiny and bright,
While octopuses juggle, oh what a sight!
With a twirl of a fin and a flip of a tail,
The underwater antics never seem stale!

The salty breeze teases our picnic spread,
While seagulls plot mischief, it's time to dread.
So guard your sandwiches, and hold on tight,
For nothing's more funny than a lunch-time flight!

Enchanted by the Expanse

Waves roll in like playful hounds,
Chasing seagulls with silly sounds.
Sand castles topple, oh what a sight,
Kingdoms built, then lost by night.

Crabs in tuxedos dance on the shore,
Declaring war in a game of chore.
Flip-flops are missing, where could they be?
Trapped in a tussle with an angry sea.

A Symphony of Shells

Shells gather round for a musical show,
Each with a secret we'd love to know.
Conch trumpets blare, while clams softly hum,
Seashells in chorus—what a fun drum!

Starfish audition for a role as a star,
Winking at waves from the rocks afar.
A sand dollar chimes like a tiny bell,
While jellyfish jiggle, all under a spell.

Ebbing Emotions

The tide comes in, then quickly goes back,
Like friends who leave with a hearty snack.
Seeking treasures, they sift and they sift,
Only to find a washed-up gift.

A fish with a grin just stole my bait,
Bubbling with laughter, it thinks it's great!
With every wave, a giggle takes flight,
Nature's own prankster, oh what a sight!

Sunkissed Reflections

Sun-bathed laughter bounces around,
Waves whisper secrets without making sound.
Flip my hat, it's flown on the breeze,
Caught by a gull, oh what a tease!

Sunscreen battles leave my nose white,
"Are you a ghost?" my friends tease in delight.
With laughter and sand, we roll on the floor,
In this golden embrace, who could ask for more?

A Bodysurf Through Silver Ribbons

Waves in laughter toss me high,
Like a fish, I try to fly.
Board shorts tied, a daring knight,
Splashing near, what a silly sight!

With every crash, a dance so bold,
My sunscreen glimmers, not much gold.
Gulls are laughing from above,
While I tumble, it's just pure love!

Riding waves like a roller coaster,
Not a pro, but a cheerful roaster.
Each wipeout brings a giggle spree,
Wet and wild, come ride with me!

So here I glide on foamy cheers,
Spinning tales with salty years.
A bodysurf beneath the sun,
Life's a splash, just having fun!

Mirrored Reflections at Twilight

Sunset paints the water's face,
Fish swim by, at quite a pace.
I squint and squabble with my hat,
Mirrored magic, a splashing spat!

Footprints draw a silly trail,
As crabs dance in a mini tale.
Seagulls gleam on a surfboard throne,
Each reflection, a giggling tone!

The sky chuckles, clouds a-float,
I strike a pose on a drifting boat.
Twilight's glow, a jester's jest,
Who knew water could be so blessed?

With friends we share this loony night,
Waves wrap us in a funny sight.
Laughter ripples, spirits rise,
Under mirrored, twinkling skies!

Gentle Lapping Against Time

Time tickles as the waves go 'splish',
I ponder life, then grab a fish.
It slips away, a sneaky tease,
While I just stand, bringing laughter to ease.

The sunset surgeon cuts the light,
And every wave plays hide and fright.
On a float, like a comfy sock,
I drift along, a floating block!

Tick-tock goes my watch of play,
Time's a prankster, gone astray.
Each lap brings stories, fun to share,
With ocean whispers in the air.

While Washington swims in politics,
I ride this wave, avoid the tricks!
A gentle flow, a brushing rhyme,
All is well, despite old time!

Tides of Peaceful Solitude

On sandy shores, I find my seat,
With snacks that taste like summer's feat.
Seashells sing a gentle tune,
While seagulls gossip 'neath the moon.

With salty hair, I try to think,
But a jellyfish floats by, I blink.
In solitude, I ponder space,
But then I trip on a crab's embrace!

The tides chuckle at my plight,
As I dance clumsily in the light.
Nature's giggles pull me near,
A symphony of fun to hear.

Here, amidst the playful brine,
I sip my drink, all's just fine.
Tides roll in, good vibes follow,
In this life, there's joy to swallow!

Ocean's Loving Arms

Waves tickle toes with a bubbly tease,
Crabs do the cha-cha, oh what a breeze!
Seagulls squawk jokes with a raucous charm,
Floating on floaties, we're safe from harm.

Sunbathers lounge with a goofy grin,
Sandy sandwiches, a feast of sin!
The ocean giggles, it splashes and plays,
As fish throw parties in a watery haze.

Life Between the Waves

Between the swells, there's mischief and fun,
A dolphin slicks by, then flips with a pun.
Surfboards collide in a splashy ballet,
Who knew the sea danced in such a way?

Jellyfish waltz with a wobbly style,
They float like balloons, making us smile.
Barnacles play quiet games of hide and seek,
While surfers contend with their floundering peak.

Saltwater Serenade

With salty air comes a whiff of delight,
Where beach balls bounce in a frothy fight.
Shells gather stories, all woven in sand,
While crabs tell tales with their little claw hand.

Waves sing ballads with a splashy refrain,
Tickling our laughter through sun and rain.
The tide's ticklish touches make everyone cheer,
As we tumble and roll, not a single worry near.

A Harbor of Hope

Boats bob along like they're ready to dance,
Their sails puffed up, giving wind a chance.
Fishermen chuckle, baiting with glee,
While mermaids giggle, 'You'll never catch me!'

In the harbor's warmth, laughter doesn't stop,
As seaweed wears hats, doing a flip and a drop.
The coastline whispers, "Join the cheeky spree,"
And we all sail forth, wild and carefree.

The Color of Calm

The waves wore sunglasses, oh so bright,
They splashed and danced, what a silly sight!
With surfboards made of jellybeans,
Sailing past in swirly, wobbly scenes.

A seagull squawked a tune with glee,
As crabs played cards, sipping on tea.
Fish in tuxedos twirled in delight,
While starfish cheered, what a goofy night!

Sandcastles giggled, built way too high,
With towers made of lollipops, oh my!
The tide rolled in with a chuckle and sigh,
As shells held secrets, winking from nearby.

Oh, what a scene, this vibrant shore,
Where laughter and fun meet forevermore.
So grab your floaties and join the spree,
In this happy place, forever carefree!

Embracing the Horizon

The sun wore flip-flops, dancing at dusk,
While rubber ducks floated, oh what a fuss!
Surfboards giggled, racing the foam,
As dolphins summoned their friends from the gloam.

A cat in a sailor hat waved hello,
While turtles practiced their slow-motion show.
Seashells chatted, gossiping with flair,
As the breeze whispered jokes, light as air.

Clouds shaped like popcorn drifted along,
As waves composed a silly sea song.
The horizon wobbled, so unsure of itself,
Like a ballerina without any help.

Crabs formed a band, clapping their claws,
While octopuses painted with no flaws.
In this haven of laughter, joy reigns supreme,
Where the horizon beckons like a whimsical dream!

Sunbeams on the Bay

Sunbeams dance upon the tide,
Seagulls squawk, they take a ride.
A crab in shorts, what a sight!
He lost a race, but feels alright.

Bubbles pop with gleeful cheer,
A fish sings tunes, oh so clear.
The dolphin does a silly flip,
While clams just sit and take a dip.

Kids build castles, watch them fall,
The tide just giggles, that's its call.
A sandcastle prince waves his hat,
As waves say, "Not so fast, chitchat!"

Sunset paints the sky so bright,
The beach is buzzing with delight.
A seagull steals a chip or two,
And leaves us laughing in the blue.

Wisps of Wind and Wonder

Whispers float on breezy trails,
As kites take off like happy snails.
The sand's a tickle, beneath our feet,
While crabs perform their funny feat.

A jellyfish drifts, without a care,
Wearing a hat, oh how it'll wear!
A seaweed dance, a silly jig,
Even the barnacles join in big!

The pelicans drop in for a snack,
While beachgoers chase after their pack.
A sunburned guy flips through the air,
And lands right there - in a wet chair!

Winds compose a breezy tune,
As sand flies by like a cartoon.
Each laugh and giggle, echoes wide,
On this kooky, silly seaside ride.

Portraits of Peace by the Coast

In shells we find our secret dreams,
A starfish grins, or so it seems.
A parrot squawks, "I'm here for chips!"
While crabs in bowties do their flips.

The sun reclines on its golden chair,
While fish gossip without a care.
A turtle sports stylish shades,
As the beach ball rolls, laughter cascades.

Seashells giggle in the breeze,
While kids chase shadows with such ease.
A young boy builds a tower high,
But waves just giggle, "Give it a try!"

Under the umbrella's shade,
Sunburned noses parade and fade.
We toast marshmallows, to the sea,
While laughter rings in harmony.

Driftwood Dreams

Driftwood claims its throne of fame,
A throne of odd, no two the same.
A fish with shades takes up the post,
While snails on parade, we cheer the most.

Flip-flops flop with every step,
A beachball goes where the wind has leapt.
We chase it down like it's the prize,
While crabs just laugh with beady eyes.

A sunburned toe is quite the scene,
With sunscreen spots like polka dots, keen!
A seagull snickers, drops a wink,
As we all ponder, "What's that stink?"

Even the tide brings funny tales,
As starfish play with jelly trails.
The shoreline laughs, in waves it glees,
While driftwood dreams float on the breeze.

Embraced by Waves

The ocean danced with glee and flair,
As seagulls squawked without a care.
I tried to swim, but got a wave,
That knocked me down—oh, how I rave!

My sandwich flew, a gull on the hunt,
It soared away; my lunch—a stunt!
I laughed and splashed, no time for shame,
For chasing snacks is all a game.

A crab wore shades; it looked so cool,
While beach balls floated—who's the fool?
With every splash, a giggle burst,
The ocean's wit—the best of first!

So here I float with friends galore,
Each wave a joke, can't ask for more.
In bubbly frolic, we all agree,
Life is better by the salty spree.

Caress of the Brine

The tide tickled my toes with glee,
While fishy whispers chanted free.
A jellyfish waved, I waved right back,
Its wobbly dance—a true knack!

With buckets in hand, we scooped for shells,
But tangled seaweed rang loud bells.
We laughed and stumbled, splashed on the way,
The ocean's mischief won the day!

A lobster danced a salsa right,
I tried to join, it gave a fright.
In crabby vogue, I lost my cool,
If swimming's magic—I'm the fool!

But as the sun began to set,
We traded tales without regret.
With salty smiles, we felt divine,
In this comical caress of brine.

Solace in the Surf

The waves giggled, in fun they crashed,
My flip-flop flew—it surely splashed!
A dolphin winked, oh what a sight,
While I flopped in foam, laughing outright!

With sandcastles built like mighty kings,
The seagulls swooped, just take my rings!
But in the chaos, with grains in hair,
I declared a truce; love's in the air!

A crab recited jokes, quite surreal,
We cheered, then rolled, our beach ball deal.
Though I fell flat, face down in the shore,
The surf, it snickered, wanting more!

In every wave, a chuckle found,
Our laughter twinkled like the sound.
Solace here most joyous and bright,
In surf's embrace, we take flight!

Lullabies of the Deep

The waves sang softly, a lullaby cheer,
While fish danced around without fear.
"Aren't you scared?" I giggled and asked,
They blinked and swam—happiness basked!

With my goggles on, I took a peek,
A clownfish giggled—what a cheek!
He swayed to the rhythm of bubbly songs,
While snoring seals hummed along like throngs.

My tailbone tingled in the ocean's grip,
A splash of water, a slippery trip!
I flopped like a seal, so out of place,
Yet, the deep held me in a warm embrace.

As night fell softly, stars all aglow,
The ocean whispered, "Come on, let's go!"
With laughter like waves, we floated away,
In lullabies of the deep, we play.

Tranquility of Distant Waves

I once met a crab who wore a hat,
He danced on the shore, so fancy and fat.
With a wink and a wave, he'd greet the fish,
"Join me for lunch? I promise it's delish!"

The seagulls laughed as they flew by high,
Stealing my fries with a swoop and a cry.
They'd trade me for chips, oh what a sight,
Who knew gulls could barter and fly with such might!

A turtle once lapped and wanted to race,
But I tripped on the sand and fell on my face.
He chuckled and cheered, "You've got speed on land!"
While I just lay there, covered in sand!

In waters so clear, my worries took flight,
With dolphins that giggled, oh what a delight.
They showed me some moves, like the twist and the spin,

But they laughed so hard, I could barely swim!

The Hush of Gentle Currents

The tide played a tune that was oh-so-sweet,
A fish wore a bowtie, now that was neat!
He crooned to the shells, serenading the shore,
While I tried to dance, but tripped on a door!

A starfish called Bob said, "Let's start a band!"
With seaweed for drums, we formed a rock stand.
But every time they'd play, a crab would complain,
"Your music is noisy, it's driving me insane!"

The waves tickled toes as they ran up the beach,
An octopus laughed as he taught me to screech.
"Just take a deep breath and open your mouth!"
But all that came out was a gobble and spout!

The sunsets would giggle, the fish joined the fray,
They flipped and they flopped in their silly ballet.
As night draped its cloak, stars came out to play,
And I dreamt of crabs hosting talent shows, hey!

Dunes of Soft Embrace

Upon the soft dunes, where whispers do twirl,
Was a clam with big dreams of being a pearl.
He'd strut on the sand in a bedazzled getup,
Thinking he'd be the next ocean celeb cup!

With sandpipers chirping their favorite hits,
I joined in the fun, doing silly skits.
But my flip flops flew off, a wild gust of winds,
And the crabs in the crowd roared with giggly grins!

A crab named Lou, with a top hat so grand,
Declared "We'll throw parties upon this fine sand!"
So we danced and we sang till the stars shone bright,
Though my dance moves looked more like a terrible fright.

As tides came to whisper a calming goodnight,
The sea laughed at us, bathed in silver moonlight.
With stars as our audience, we took our last bow,
Silly beach creatures, oh what a wow!

Waves of Comforting Caress

A walrus named Greg wore a swimsuit of plaid,
He sunbathed with style, the coolest I've had!
But he slipped on a wave and landed with BOOM,
Sent splashes, oh splashes, right into the room!

While jellyfish floated and lit up the night,
They laughed at my flip as I tried to take flight.
"Don't dance with the tide! You're out of your league!"
But I giggled and wiggled, thought it was great league!

A turtle in shades sipped a drink on the shore,
"Just chill with the tides, don't worry, explore!"
With a smile on his face and a straw in his shell,
He showed me the tricks of the ocean so well.

As waves wrapped around, a soft lullaby,
I felt all my worries just ebb and flow by.
With laughter and joy, I embraced what came,
In this wacky wild ocean, nothing's the same!

Moonlit Waters

Bobbing boats sing out the tune,
A fish jumps up, it's a little rude.
The moon laughs loud, a silver prize,
As seagulls squawk, and sailors rise.

Flip-flops splashing, laughter's sound,
A crab scuttles, chaos abound.
Chasing shadows, dodging waves,
What a night for silly braves!

With marshmallow clouds and jellyfish,
We toast to dreams and silly wishes.
A dolphin cracks a cheeky grin,
Who knew the ocean could be such sin?

As tides respond with playful grins,
We dance beneath as the fun begins.
With every wave, we sail and leap,
In laughter's lap, we dive so deep.

Surrender to the Tide

Floating flippers, splash and swirl,
A seagull dances, a jolly twirl.
Sandcastles crumble like icing cakes,
With every wave, the shoreline shakes.

A trio of turtles race on by,
With jelly beans up in the sky.
We toss out snacks to fishy friends,
Hoping their nibbling never ends.

In goofy goggles and bright pink fins,
We dip our toes, let the fun begin.
As crabs join in with a funky beat,
Our silly antics can't be beat!

With every roll and splashy slide,
We find our joy, and there's no pride.
Just simple laughter in tidal rhymes,
Forever joy, in splashing times.

A Dance of Salt and Wind

Whirling kites against blue skies,
The sun winks down, mischief flies.
A sea breeze teases hair askew,
As the surf sings out, 'Surprise, it's you!'

A few brave souls jump in for fun,
But chilly waves can make you run.
"Catch me if you can!" the tide will say,
As sand flies up in a beach ballet.

The gulls and kids, a merry mix,
In a game of tag with salty tricks.
A flip, a flop, and down we go,
With laughter echoing, hearts aglow.

As dusk paints shades of golden glow,
We dance our last in the ebb and flow.
With weary bones, we say goodbye,
To salt and wind beneath the sky.

Serenity Among the Swells

On floating logs, we set our course,
With marshmallows on hand, of course.
A splash here and a giggle there,
All join to float this sea of flair.

Our rubber ducks yes, they parade,
Amidst the waves, we aren't afraid.
With clumsy strokes, we arm and leg,
"Look out!" we shout, "I might just beg!"

A gentle breeze lifts spirits high,
As fishy friends flit and fly.
The salt and sand, a tickly fate,
And laughter's giggle, really great!

As the sun dips low, we wave goodnight,
In dreams we'll dance by moonlight bright.
For in this space, so wild and free,
Joy's true essence is all we see.

The Quiet Call of the Coast

The waves roll in with a laugh,
They tease each shell on the sand.
Seagulls squawk a silly jest,
While kids build castles quite unplanned.

A crab in shorts scuttles by,
Waving claws like a silly dance.
Sandcastles toppling like dreams,
As soon as the tide takes its chance.

A beach ball flies, a wild loop,
Lands smack on a sunbather's hat.
Giggles mix with salty air,
As folks yelp at the flat attack.

With sunscreen smeared on every face,
And umbrellas that just won't stay put.
The coast is a funhouse today,
Where laughter takes root like a foot.

A Refuge Beneath the Waves

Flipping flippers like they own,
Fish parade in fancy attire.
A dolphin makes a cheeky face,
While a clownfish vies for the choir.

Octopuses juggle their snacks,
With eight arms, they steal the show.
"Hey, watch this!" one shouts with glee,
As a starfish shouts, "Just let it go!"

Sea urchins roll in, spined with pride,
Claiming turf like a bouncer tall.
"Not on my watch!" they bravely scoff,
As the tide dares them to a ball.

Anemones wave like party girls,
In dressings of color and flair.
With bubbles and giggles, all around,
Who needs a reason for a fair?

Caressing Breezes

A gust of wind with a tickling tease,
Swirls through hair like a playful dance.
Kites take flight with a mischievous grin,
And kids run chasing, lost in a trance.

Sand flies up in a cheeky shower,
As hats go bouncing, no need to fret.
"Catch my chapeau!" shouts a merry mom,
While dad throws a fit with a sudsy net.

Lighthearted clouds drift with the breeze,
Wishing sunscreen was in their patch.
"Who wore it better?" they giggle and tease,
While the sun just shakes its hot batch.

A picnic's laid, ants come in droves,
Helping themselves to the feast of delights.
With laughter and crumbs, they dance on the scene,
Stealing the show on kite-flying nights.

Murmurs in the Mist

At dawn, the mist hugs the shore,
Like a grandpa with stories untold.
Whispers of fish fly through the air,
"Fetch the nets, time to be bold!"

A seal pops up with a wink and nod,
Sending ripples of laughter around.
"Be careful, I'm slippery!" he shouts with glee,
Making waves with a comic sound.

Foghorns blare from some distant boats,
Sailing off like they're in a race.
"Not today!" laughs the tide cheekily,
As it rolls back with a splashing grace.

The gulls join in for a sing-a-long,
Flapping wings to a wacky beat.
With fish as the punchline, they laugh it up,
In morning's mist, life tastes so sweet.

Seashell Whispers

A seashell spoke to me today,
It said, "Please don't let me stray!"
I laughed and tossed it with a grin,
Back to the waves, let the fun begin!

Mollusks party on ocean floors,
While crabs practice their dance on shores.
With each wave, a joke is told,
Ocean humor never grows old!

Starfish giggle in the tide,
As surfboards wipe out, oh what a ride!
Seashells chuckle in the sand,
It's a playful, aquatic wonderland!

I picked up a shell, it said "Ouch!"
Turns out it wasn't just a couch!
Anemones wave like silly fans,
All while fish form synchronized plans!

Cloaked in Blue Serenity

Waves in sparkly blue attire,
They dance and swirl, full of desire.
A dolphin jumped, with a splash,
As seagulls squawked, "Let's make a big splash!"

The ocean wore its best big grin,
With barnacles that tickle your chin.
Fish in tuxedos waltzed so fine,
While coral reefs brewed their own wine!

Lobsters in shades poolside reclined,
They laughed at the antics of the unwinded.
Jellyfish floated with glimmering style,
Synced up to the beat of the ocean's smile!

Mermaids twisted their tresses in fun,
While crabs debated who had won.
With waves like laughter around us all,
Every splash is another laugh call!

Dunes and Delicacies

Sandcastle chefs cooking up treats,
With seashells serving delicious sweets.
Starfish topped with a sprinkle of glee,
As crabs pranced like they were at a spree!

Dune bunnies doing the tango,
As waves clap like they're at a fandango.
The ocean's buffet is great and vast,
Where even the clams wear a party cast!

There's sifting sugar from the sky,
But watch out for the gulls that fly!
In this sandy kitchen, laughter is key,
Where the bites are as big as the sea!

With waves that wink and sand that grins,
Each meal's a race — let the fun begin!
Dishes drift like music notes,
While the tide hums tunes from sun-kissed boats!

Touch of the Tide

Every tide has a secret to share,
Like octopuses with multi-colored flair.
They play peek-a-boo with sand and light,
Causing giggles in the morning bright!

The ripples dance with a joyful sound,
Tickling toes that are beach-bound.
A whale just told a whale of a tale,
Of mermaid teas in a seaweed sail!

Waves crash high and plop down low,
Inviting clams for the evening show.
Oysters chuckle, trying to rhyme,
Their shells clapping in perfect time!

With each splash comes a hearty cheer,
For the joys that the ocean holds dear.
So join the dance with the sand and brine,
Where laughter and tides happily intertwine!

Whispers of Tidal Kisses

A wave curled up to say hello,
With a splash it said, 'You've got to go!'
It tickled my toes, so playful it seemed,
As I laughed out loud, I hardly dreamed.

Fish swam by with a wink and a grin,
Said, 'Why dive in? Just come for a spin!'
They danced in circles, a watery jig,
While I tried to keep up, not doing too big.

Seagulls overhead cawed jokes a'plenty,
'Pick up a shell, it's totally trendy!'
But I tripped on sand, flew like a kite,
Sandy and soggy, what a sight!

Finally, the tide pulled back with a laugh,
It took my hat, said, 'This is my bath!'
As it tumbled away in frothy delight,
I waved goodbye, and laughed at the sight.

Ocean's Velvet Touch

The water was calm, like a cozy quilt,
I dropped my ice cream—oh, what a wilt!
Seashells laughed as they witnessed the fall,
'You're better off with us, come take a stall!'

Waves giggled softly as they rolled on by,
Whispering secrets of the fish who fly.
They joked of dolphins who wore bright bow ties,
Making the drab beach laugh 'till it cries.

Crabs did the cha-cha, moving with flair,
While I stumbled again, legs caught in a snare.
'Balance, my friend,' said a sardine in blue,
As I danced on the shore, what else could I do?

The breeze chuckled softly, a tickle so light,
It ruffled my hair, 'Keep cozy, it's right!'
But I lost my glasses, oh what a blunder,
'You'll find new views!' it laughed in my wonder!

Embrace of Salty Breezes

The salty air tickled my nose,
While hermit crabs danced in their clothes.
I joined their parade, thought I was slick,
'Til I slipped on a shell—oh, what a trick!

Waves whispered jokes that flew out to shore,
'Did you hear the one about a crab who wanted more?'
It dreamt of being a mighty blue whale,
But all it could manage was a wobbly sail.

A treasure chest laughed, filled with old shoes,
'These don't fit, but the ocean can't lose!'
The gulls were my audience, cawing with glee,
As I tried to juggle, a split at my knee.

At sunset, the tide pulled back with a cheer,
'Don't worry, my friend! The fun's always near!'
So I waved at the sea, with a grin on my face,
In this wacky grand show, I found my place.

Currents of Serenity

In the calm, there's laughter, I swear it's true,
The waves are all chatting, in shades of blue.
Each flip of a fin brings giggles galore,
While seahorses play on the ocean floor.

I joined in their fun, tried to swim with a splash,
But a surfboard said, 'Whoa! You're quite the crash!'
It rolled with a chuckle, my balance was lame,
'Being a fish is just more of a game!'

The octopus winked, flipping off a shell,
'You're getting the hang of it! Do tell, do tell!'
I squealed with delight, feeling brave and bold,
While jellyfish giggled at the tales I told.

The tide swayed gently, a soft, sweet embrace,
While I juggled starfish, lost in the chase.
The ocean laughed, full of mirth and delight,
In these currents of joy, the world felt so right.

Harmony with the Horizon

Waves tickle toes with a splash,
Seagulls swoop in for a snack.
Kids scream loud as they dash,
While sand castles start to crack.

Flip-flops fly like flying fish,
Sunburns come with every wish.
Laughter echoes in the air,
As sunscreen meets a vacant chair.

Buckets filled with seashell finds,
Sandwich crumbs left behind.
Tide pulls back with a cheeky grin,
As we dance in the salty wind.

Ice cream drips down chins so neat,
Seagulls eye the tasty treat.
Every moment is a delight,
Underneath that sun so bright.

Calm after the Storm

Clouds have fled, and smiles return,
Puddles shimmer, kids take turns.
Rubber ducks sail on board,
While laughter becomes the reward.

Waves once wild, now giggle soft,
As boats rock gently aloft.
Sunscreen greets a wary breeze,
With flip-flops dancing on their knees.

Footprints lead to hidden treasures,
Tide pools filled with slimy pleasures.
Plastic shovels dig for gold,
As sassy snails strike poses bold.

Chums create a bucket brigade,
Building walls that will not fade.
Egrets strut in purest style,
As beach towels take a well-earned trial.

Reclamation of the Coastline

Sand dunes shift with youthful glee,
Boys dig deep to unearth a spree.
Mysterious shells that wink and smile,
Hope they don't end their days in a pile.

Whispers of ocean tales unfold,
Every beachcomber's eye is bold.
Starfish posing as nature's art,
While crabs march in a flimsy cart.

Kites soar high like ideas gone mad,
They twist and twirl, it's quite a fad.
Wind whispers secrets to the shore,
As laughter reigns forever more.

Belly flops from brave little beans,
They try to impress with drippy scenes.
A grand parade of beachside fun,
Until the ice cream has all gone.

Crashing Comfort

Waves crash in a playful splash,
Where surfboards wobble and dash.
Seagulls squabble over snacks,
As friends relax with chilled six packs.

Warm sun melts any chilly mood,
While tides dance in joyful brood.
Beach balls fly like goofy spies,
Dodging shadows of passing guys.

Sun hats tipped at a funny angle,
As tan lines become the local dangle.
Splash fight erupts like laughter in air,
Wet clothes, but nobody cares.

Sandman builds a castle so grand,
Only to be humbled by a child's hand.
All around, the joy is loud,
In this beachside, merry crowd.

Surf and Solitude

Waves crash and splatter, like fish in a fight,
My board's a strange vehicle, not quite polite.
I'm balancing wobbly, feeling quite spry,
Until I meet the ocean, and say my goodbye.

Seagulls are laughing, they know all my tricks,
While I'm slipping and sliding, like a clown on cool bricks.
With sand in my shorts and salt in my hair,
My dignity floats off, like a boat with no care.

The sun's high above, like a bright shining bulb,
The waves throw a party, chaos to my lobe.
I ride with the tide, or I fall with a splash,
Laughing at the ocean, it's quite the bold clash.

But as the tide ebbs, I'll stand tall and proud,
With tales of my tumbles to share with the crowd.
For every wipeout, there's a giggle too,
In this salty ballet, where I'm the star, who knew?

Heartbeats Among the Ripples

Floating like jelly, my heart skips a beat,
While dodging the waves, they whisper so sweet.
A dolphin approaches, all smiles and glee,
I swear he just winked, is he flirting with me?

With foam on my face, I giggle and splash,
A seaweed surprise makes my hairstyle a crash.
The fish circle 'round, like they want a part,
In this dance of the tides, I'll play the odd heart.

Oh bubbles arise, like champagne in the sun,
Each burst is a laughter, we're having such fun.
The crabs throw a dance-off, I try to keep pace,
But a slip and a trip, ends in sand on my face.

But through all the blunders, I'll cherish the thrill,
As heartbeats are mingled with the ocean's chill.
So here's to the laughter, in waves that I chase,
For every tiny ripple, I'm lost in their grace.

Memories Adrift

In my boat of old memories, I float and I sway,
With each gentle wave, they get tossed and play.
A jellyfish pops by, with a grin on his face,
I'm certain he's judging my nautical grace.

The tides whisper tales of mischief and fun,
Like the time I brought snacks to a stingray run.
They flocked for my goodies, I lost track of time,
Now my sandwiches float, like a soggy soft rhyme.

Seagulls are gossiping, over my head,
"Did you hear about the swimmer? He got caught in a thread!"
I chuckle and watch as the waves dance and tease,
With a throwback to days when I mastered the seas.

As I sail through the echoes of what used to be,
I snort at my blunders, the vainness of me.
With laughter, I paddle, adrift and set free,
For these memories float like the jellyfish, see?

Tidal Embrace

The tide rolls in with a playful wink,
While I hold my breath and start to rethink.
With foam all around, I'm a sight to behold,
Is it me or the waves who are really so bold?

A wave closes in, I try to look cool,
But I'm more like a seal than the chic kind of fool.
Among all these splashes, I'll flounder, I vow,
As the ocean holds me, takes bows, and says "wow!"

The mermaids all giggle, they shake their long hair,
They toss me a bubble, while taking a dare.
I juggle my laughter with each splash I face,
In this merry mad dance of the wild, watery space.

With each mischievous wave, I'm swept off my feet,
But I'll wave back at chaos, this rhythm's so sweet.
In the tidal embrace, we create quite a scene,
For laughter's the treasure, in ocean's sheen.

The Calm Between Storms

In stillness where waves take a nap,
Seagulls dance in a feathered flap.
Crabs in tuxedos strut with style,
While fish in flip-flops swim a mile.

A dolphin winks, says, "Join my team!"
But all I have is a soggy dream.
The wind whispers jokes to the shore,
While sandcastles giggle, wanting more!

Under puffy clouds like giant cakes,
I spot a whale making fishy flakes.
A beach ball rolls, then shouts, "Whee!"
The sun shares secrets with a bumblebee!

Then suddenly, a storm's in the trick,
But the sea just laughs, saying, "Not so quick!"
With a wink and wave, it turns back tame,
And I'm left wondering, who's to blame?

Moonlit Cradle of the Surf

The moon plays peekaboo with the tide,
While mermaids ride a wave for a glide.
Crabs in disco balls wear shades so bright,
Dancing under stars, what a silly sight!

Fish sporting mustaches sing a tune,
As starfish lounge, soaking up the moon.
A clam with a crown catches dreamy rays,
While seashells gossip about their days.

Jellyfish twirl in a wobbly ball,
Every splash sends the seaweed to fall.
A dolphin jokes, "Who needs a car?
When you can ride waves and shoot for the stars!"

As night wraps up in a fluffy quilt,
The ocean chuckles with a wink built.
Pearls giggle softly, under the fun,
In this moonlit cradle, we're never done.

A Gentle Respite by Ocean's Edge

Sandy toes and laughter in the breeze,
Giggles echo like buzzing bees.
The tide rolls in, brings its tickling play,
And seaside snacks that want to stay!

Children build towers, their castles of joy,
While sandmen dance with a goofy ploy.
An octopus juggles shells with grace,
While crabs take selfies, what a weird place!

A breeze whispers secrets so absurd,
While fish debate who's heard what word.
Pelicans dive into a splashy cheer,
Jumping on waves, full of glee and beer!

As day melts into shades of warm hue,
Seashells chuckle while we bid adieu.
The ocean winks, saying, "Come back soon,
We're here for fun, beneath the bright moon!"

Secrets of the Shimmering Tide

Beneath the glimmer, there's laughter so grand,
With crabs in tuxes forming a band.
Fish in bow ties serve tea with flair,
While seagulls swap tales of fishy air!

Salty breeze carries whispers of glee,
As the ocean spins a tale for me.
"Dive right in, let's join the fun,
You'll swim with dolphins before you're done!"

Starfish with sunglasses basking in light,
Counting all the ripples that splash with delight.
The tide rolls in, with a giggly fling,
Making seashells dance to the tunes they sing!

With every wave, a joke in disguise,
Sea turtles travel with wondering eyes.
So I tip my hat, give the ocean a wink,
For every splash tells a funny old link.

Currents of Comfort

Waves tickle toes, oh what a treat,
A jellyfish dance, not so discreet.
Sand flies like confetti, all around,
Did I really just lose that sandwich I found?

Seagulls squawk loudly, demanding a fry,
As I toss them my lunch, they laugh at my sigh.
A swim with the fish, I do a neat flop,
But next, I just sink like a stone from the top.

The tide brings my hat, but my friend steals the rest,
That crab on my leg seems to think he's the best.
Sunburned and silly, I flop down in chairs,
With laughter and snacks, we forget all our cares.

Here in the Harbor

In the harbor, boats snicker like pals,
One's lost its anchor, another's got gales.
Fishermen casting, tangled in lines,
Oh look, there goes Bob with his sandwich of pines!

A dolphin pops up, doing flips in the spray,
Riding the waves, what a comical play!
But wait, what's that? A seal's stealing flair,
He's wearing my hat—now that's just not fair!

Picnics unfold, and seagulls plot schemes,
One swoops down, caught me in my daydreams.
Grabbing my fries with a side of my smile,
I chase him away, it's worth the while!

Unraveling at Dusk

As the sun dips low, we splash and we squeal,
But oh, what's this? I tripped on a wheel.
Giggling crabs gather, they're plotting a coup,
They challenge my balance, 'Can you dance too?'

Waves tickling my ankles, I wiggle and squirm,
Caught in their laughter, I've lost all my charm.
Fish jump for joy, while I stumble and glide,
A flip that goes wrong with a splash, but I'm pride!

The sun paints the sky with a palette of fun,
While moonlight comes dancing, day's over, we run.
With stars overhead, we still hear the giggles,
Living it up with our squishy, wet jiggles!

Sandcastle Heartbeats

With buckets and shovels, we dig in a race,
Building a castle that's really a space.
Moats filled with giggles, drawbridges of cheer,
But watch out for that wave, it's drawing near!

A knight made of shells gets ready for battle,
But as it starts raining, we jump back and prattle.
"Execute plan 'Sandy'!" one kid yells aloud,
We stampede for cover, a wild, frantic crowd!

At last we emerge, soaked to the bone,
Our castle's collapsed, but we still feel at home.
With laughter and sand, our spirits ignite,
We'll build it again, right by moon's lovely light!

Echoes of Warm Waters

Waves giggle as they crash,
Tickling toes with a splash.
Seagulls dive for a snack,
Warning fish to watch their back.

Floating toys dance on the tide,
Rubber duckies go for a ride.
Sunburned sunbathers say,
"Next time, we'll bring shade all day!"

A crab dons shades, looks so cool,
He struts around like a fool.
Shells whisper secrets out loud,
While beach balls bounce, so proud.

Swimmers laugh with mouths full of sand,
As sandcastles fall by hand.
Even dolphins try to tease,
With flips that aim to please.

Gentle Hands of the Horizon

Waves tiptoe in for a kiss,
Sandy footprints mark bliss.
A pelican starts to dance,
Wobbling like he lost his pants.

Seashells giggle, having fun,
Mocking crabs on the run.
Sunlit surfers wipe out fast,
Splashing onlookers with a blast.

The tide's rhythm makes us sway,
As munching whales steal the day.
Plankton parties in the dark,
Rave lights flicker, what a spark!

Seagulls swoop with a caw,
Stealing fries, breaking the law.
The ocean sings—oh so free,
In its quirky jubilee.

Horizons in Harmony

Bubbles rise, tickling the nose,
As playful fish strike silly poses.
An octopus shows us his flair,
With eight arms, he spins through air.

The wind blows hats off happy heads,
Beachgoers dive for their dreads.
The tide pulls in with a wink,
While the sun takes a moment to think.

Crabby critters march in style,
Making crowds stop for a while.
Turtles glide, slow but wise,
With sunglasses hiding their eyes.

Kids giggle, splashing around,
While soggy sandwiches hit the ground.
Splashing laughter fills the bay,
As sandy snacks are on display.

Nautical Nurturing

A rubber shark takes a swim,
Chasing waves at the whim.
Mermaids giggle under the sun,
While their clam shell phones are fun.

A sailboat spills its lunch,
As gulls dive in for a crunch.
Tide pools are a circus show,
Where the sea stars put on a glow.

Paddleboards race like mad,
While jellyfish look quite sad.
A fishy band sings a tune,
Swishing fins to the moon.

The ocean's mood is cheeky and bright,
As the sunset fades from sight.
In this world where laughter thrives,
Nature gives a high-five!

Caresses from the Horizon's Edge

Waves tickle my toes with delight,
They're slippery little gremlins tonight!
Seagulls squawk with a cheeky grin,
Stealing snacks, oh, where do I begin?

The sun suits up in golden rays,
While I attempt to dance, a clumsy gaze.
A crab scuttles off, it thinks it's grand,
"Don't leave me behind!" I plea, in the sand.

Saltwater splashes, a fresh, wet hug,
Tangled up in seaweed, snug as a bug.
I try to surf on a foam-filled wave,
But end up swallowed—what a splashy grave!

With flip-flops flying, I sprint to safety,
Chasing after my hat, quick and hasty.
The beach is magic, a silly retreat,
Where laughter meets waves in a rhythm so sweet.

Lullabies of the Crescent Tide

The moon lulls the waves into cozy dreams,
While I juggle shells, or so it seems.
A fish jumps high, makes quite the scene,
Splashing my snack—oh, what a cuisine!

Stars twinkle down with a giggle, so bright,
Their constellations form a comical sight.
A dolphin winks, does a dance, oh dear,
I join in with flippers, fueled by cheer!

The tide rolls in with a gentle chuckle,
A jellyfish wobbles, a big squishy buckle.
With every wave, I just can't resist,
Finding odd treasures in a sea-salted mist.

As moonbeams tumble on sands so warm,
I stumble and trip, amidst the charm.
With laughter resounding, I shout, "What fun!"
This moonlit party has only begun!

A Dance with the Water's Soul

Barefoot, I tango on the tide's soft edge,
Where water meets sand—it's like a pledge.
Fish swim by with a curious stare,
"Join us!" they chime, "We won't even care!"

The crabs join in with a clattering beat,
While I spin round, feeling light on my feet.
They pinch my toe, oh, what a prank,
Laughing and dancing with a big, bold tank!

Seashells clap in a rhythmic bray,
Their colors twinkling in a nautical ballet.
I take a bow, in the ocean's vast hall,
And trip on a wave, I'm bound to fall!

But the water just giggles, rolls with glee,
"Come on back and dance, you silly bee!"
So here I whirl in this fresh, salty art,
With my dance partner, nature, holding my heart!

Harmonies of Shell and Sand

On the shore, I sing to the shells so bright,
They echo my tune, what a silly sight!
A sea star joins, it waves with flair,
I take a bow; it's quite the rare affair.

Waves join in, clapping their foamy hands,
Telling me tales of faraway lands.
A crab with a tambourine starts to sway,
Rocking out with me—it's a crustacean play!

The sand tickles my toes, plays a prank,
While I spin and laugh, feeling cheeky and frank.
A beach ball bounces into the show,
Its roundness championing the fun to flow.

With each joyous note, the sky starts to glow,
As the sun takes a bow for the evening's encore.
Together we sing till the stars rise anew,
In the harmonies spun from the ocean's deep blue!

Ocean's Warmest Hug

The waves roll in like a laughing friend,
Chasing my toes, hoping to blend.
Seagulls squawk, like they own the vibe,
Stealing my sandwich — oh, how they jibe!

Sunshine is a blanket, cozy and bright,
But I burn like a lobster—what a fright!
My hat flies away with a cheeky breeze,
The ocean plays tricks, oh, such a tease!

Flip-flops are flying, it's quite the scene,
As I trip on the sand, looking so keen.
With laughter all around, we make a splash,
Life's too short not to gallop and dash!

Now I wear a crab as my quirky crown,
He pinches my ear, but I don't drown!
A dance with the tide, a splash and a giggle,
In this warm hug, I can't help but wiggle!

Melodies of the Shore

Shells sing songs as they dance in the foam,
Grains of sand make their way to my home.
The crab on the rock has a snappy tune,
While fish throw a party — quite the festoon!

With every wave's crash, there's laughter galore,
Jumping and dodging, I'm never a bore.
The beach ball bounces like a hyper pup,
While my cousin belly flops, oh, what a sup!

The sun starts to set, painting skies so pink,
But watch for the seagulls — they sure do stink!
Dinner's in the offing, they smell our fries,
They swoop down to steal, those crafty guys!

But as night falls softly, the laughter will flow,
With stories of crabs that make funny show.
The ocean keeps singing, a lullaby tune,
While we giggle and speak to the shimmering moon!

Beneath the Azure Sky

Under the sky so brilliantly blue,
We paddle and splash, what else can we do?
A dolphin appears, trying to sing,
But all that we hear is him blowing a ring!

Mermaids peek out, they're braiding their hair,
But one gets entangled, what a messy affair!
We chuckle as she gives a flustered glance,
While jellyfish jive in a bizarre dance!

The sandcastle challenge brings giggles and cheer,
As everyone joins, no one shows fear.
Shells become shovels, it's utter delight,
Until the tide comes in — oh, what a fright!

But in this wild moment, we'll never back down,
Enjoying the laughter, rejoicing the sound.
The sun dips away, we'll treasure this day,
Where fun meets the waves in the most silly way!

Dreaming with the Dunes

In the dunes, we tumble, oh what a sight,
Sand all in my hair, but it feels just right.
A race with the wind, I'm sure I can win,
But trip on a flip-flop — oh well, where to begin?

The kites in the sky seem to giggle and tease,
As they dance through the air with the playful breeze.
I sip on my drink, but it's tipped on my shirt,
Turns out I'm not graceful — who knew this would hurt?

Crickets are chirping their nighttime song,
While I tell ghost stories, but get them all wrong.
A raccoon joins in, peeking with glee,
To grab my snacks — what's that, one for me?

As we lay on the sand, dolphins take flight,
Our dreams are all mixed in this magical night.
Laughs surround us, as the stars start to glow,
In the wild, wacky tales of the evening's show!

www.ingramcontent.com/pod-product-compliance
Lightning Source LLC
Chambersburg PA
CBHW070310120526
44590CB00017B/2618